XAMonline, Inc.
25 First Street, Suite 106
Cambridge, MA 02141
Toll Free: 1-800-509-4128
Email: info@xamonline.com
Web: www.xamonline.com
Fax: 1-617-583-5552

Library of Congress Cataloging-in-Publication Data

Wynne, Sharon A.
   PRAXIS ParaPro Assessment 0755 Practice Test 1: Teacher Certification /
   Sharon A. Wynne. -1st ed.
   ISBN: 978-1-60787-127-9
   1. PRAXIS ParaPro Assessment 0755 Practice Test 1   2. Study Guides
   3. PRAXIS   4. Teachers' Certification & Licensure   5. Careers

Disclaimer:
The opinions expressed in this publication are the sole works of XAMonline and were created
independently from the National Education Association, Educational Testing Service, or any
State Department of Education, National Evaluation Systems or other testing affiliates.

Between the time of publication and printing, state specific standards as well as testing
formats and website information may change that is not included in part or in whole within this
product. Sample test questions are developed by XAMonline and reflect similar content as on
real tests; however, they are not former tests. XAMonline assembles content that aligns with
state standards but makes no claims nor guarantees teacher candidates a passing score.
Numerical scores are determined by testing companies such as NES or ETS and then are
compared with individual state standards. A passing score varies from state to state.

Printed in the United States of America   œ-1
PRAXIS ParaPro Assessment 0755 Practice Test 1
ISBN: 978-1-60787-127-9

READING

Directions: Reading the following passage and answer questions 1-3.

Oberlin, Ohio, is located south of Lake Eerie and about 40 miles east of Toledo, Ohio. Oberlin, Ohio, is home to about 8,000 residents who find it to be a lovely place to call home. It is also home to Oberlin College. Oberlin College is a private liberal arts school that was established on September 2, 1833. Oberlin is home to approximately 2,850 students and 1,058 staff members. Perhaps it is most notably known for being the first college in the United States to regularly admit African-American students in 1835. In 1837, Oberlin College became one of the first co-educational colleges when it admitted four women, Mary Kellogg, Mary Caroline Rudd, Mary Hosfor, and Elizabeth Prall. Consequently, in 1841 it was one of the first colleges to confer degrees on women when they graduated four years later.

1. **What is the main idea of the above passage?**
   (Average) (Skill 1.1)

   A. Oberlin, Ohio, is a lovely place to live

   B. Oberlin College is a private liberal arts school

   C. Oberlin College is well known for its many firsts

   D. Oberlin College was one of the first schools to grant degrees to women

2. **What is the author's purpose?**
   (Rigorous) (Skill 1.1)

   A. To inform

   B. To entertain

   C. To describe

   D. To narrate

3. **Which detail supports the idea that Oberlin College was a pioneer in the area of equal rights for women? (Rigorous) (Skill 1.3)**

   A. Oberlin college became one of the first co-educational colleges when it admitted four women

   B. Mary Kellogg attended Oberlin college

   C. Mary Hosfor received a degree from Oberlin College in 1841

   D. Oberlin College began to regularly admit African-Americans n 1835

Directions: Read the following passage and answer question 4.

Many people say that the story *The Ugly Duckling* mirrors Hans Christian Andersen's childhood. He was an odd child and did not fit in well with other children. Hans was often older than other children and because of this felt alienated. He was interested in the stage and visited the playhouse outside of Copenhagen with his father. However, eventually he was sent away to a boarding school. His experience there was dreadful. He lived with the schoolmaster where he was abused. The headmaster had said it was a way to improve his character.

4. **Which detail supports the main idea, "Hans Christian Andersen had a difficult childhood"? (Rigorous) (Skill 1.2)**

   A. Hans Christian Andersen's headmaster abused him

   B. Hans' life mirrored that of *The Ugly Duckling*

   C. Hans was often older than other children

   D. Hans enjoyed the theatre as a child

5. A student writes an essay that shows the similarities and differences between a book and a movie of the same title. What type of essay is it?
(Easy) (Skill 1.3)

  A. Classification

  B. Compare and contrast

  C. Cause and effect

  D. Statement support

6. In Writer's Workshop students are asked to write a personal narrative. How should their writing be organized?
(Average) (Skill 1.3)

  A. Statement support

  B. Compare and contrast

  C. Sequence of events

  D. Classification

7. Engineers thought it would be difficult to *construct* the Golden Gate Bridge because of the weather conditions and the ocean currents that exist in California.
(Easy) (Skill 1.4)

What does the word *construct* mean in the sentence above?

  A. Drive across

  B. Close down

  C. Make longer

  D. Build or create

8. If you have had a cough for a long time, it is said to be:
(Rigorous) (Skill 1.4)

  A. Chronic

  B. Prescriptive

  C. Contagious

  D. Malicious

Time seemed to be passing so slowly. Leslie looked at the clock for at least the hundredth time in the past hour. She turned back and looked the other way. Soon this became uncomfortable too and she turned and laid on her back. This position also didn't feel right so she turned back toward the clock. Twenty minutes had passed. "Umph," Leslie grunted closing her eyes again.

9. **From Leslie's actions we can determine that**
   (Average) (Skill 1.5)

   A. Leslie is laying on the beach somewhere

   B. Leslie is at the doctor's office waiting her turn

   C. Leslie is excited about an upcoming event

   D. Leslie is having a difficult time sleeping

Molly slid into her gorgeous dress. She had imagined this day since she was a young girl living in Hartford, Connecticut. Checking herself in the mirror one last time, she decided that this was as good as it was going to get. Her hair was perfect, just the way she had imagined—the hairdresser had definitely earned her fee this morning. As did the make-up specialist Molly thought to herself as she examined her face in the mirror. Then she heard the anthem of the orchestra. She turned from the mirror and headed toward the aisle.

10. **It can be inferred from the passage above that Molly is:**
    (Average) (Skill 1.5)

    A. A runway model

    B. About to get married

    C. Shopping at a store

    D. A Broadway performer

11. **All of the following statements are opinions** *EXCEPT* *(Average) (Skill 1.6)*

   A. Mrs. Krissy is the best teacher at Ringdale Elementary School

   B. The third grade test is difficult for the students

   C. Ringdale Elementary School hasn't been around that long

   D. There are 853 students at Ringdale Elementary School

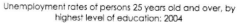

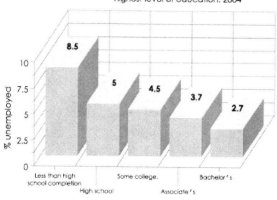

Highest level of education

U.S. Department of Labor, Bureau of Labor Statistics, Office of Employment and Unemployment Statistics, Current Population Survey (CPS), 2004.

12. **According to the graph, what group of people made up the largest percentage of the unemployed in 2004?** *(Average) (Skill 1.7)*

   A. Those who did not complete High School

   B. Those who completed High School

   C. Those who have taken some college credit

   D. Those who possess a Bachelor's degree

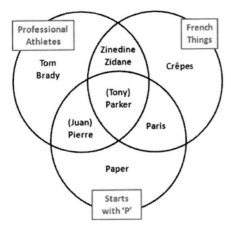

Sample Venn Diagram

13. **According to the Venn Diagram, what is true about "Paris"?**
(Rigorous) (Skill 1.7)

A. It starts with "P"

B. It is a French Thing

C. It is the name of a professional athlete

D. It starts with "P" and is a French Thing

14. **According to the Venn Diagram, what fits within all three categories?**
(Rigorous) (Skill 1.7)

A   Tony Parker

B   Zinedine Zidane

C   Juan Pierre

D   Paris

15. **A student is reading and gets stuck on the word *sure*. All of the following are good ways to help the student decode the word EXCEPT**
(Average) (Skill 2.1)

A. Have the student sound it out

B. Have the student skip the word and come back

C. Tell the student is rhymes with *lure*

D. Tell the student that *ur* makes the *er* sound

16. **How many syllables does the word *chocolate* have?**
(Easy) (Skill 2.1)

A. 1

B. 2

C. 3

D. 4

17. **How does adding the prefix *dis-* to the word *continue*, change its meaning?**
(Average) (Skill 2.2)

A. It now means "to continue later"

B. It now means "to do again"

C. It now means "to not continue"

D   It doesn't change the meaning

18. **Which combination of words produces an irregular contraction?**
(Average) (Skill 2.2)

A. did + not

B. you + are

C. I + will

D. will + not

19. **Besides teaching scientific methods and information, what might be a good lesson to teach along with a book about photosynthesis?**
(Rigorous) (Skill 2.2)

A. The first photograph taken

B. The root –photo- means light

C. The food chain

D. The letter /ph/ make the "f" sound

20. **A student reads the sentence, "The boy saw a worm in the ground," and says "The boy saw a worm in the grass." What might you say to the student as a paraprofessional?**
(Rigorous) (Skill 2.3)

A. "You said grass. Look at this word and tell me why it can't be grass."

B. "Look at this word again [pointing to ground]. What sound does this word begin with?"

C. "What vowels do you see in this word? [pointing to ground]"

D. "Where is another place you might see a worm?"

21. **What is a synonym for the word "fast"?**
(Easy) (Skill 2.4)

A. Slow

B. Last

C. Speedy

D. Quickly

22. **Which word belongs in the blank?**
    (Easy) (Skill 2.4)

    Some people like to paint _____ houses garish colors.

    A. they're

    B. there

    C. their

    D. None of these work

23. **What is the best strategy to help students alphabetize words?**
    (Rigorous) (Skill 2.5)

    A. Have students write random words in alphabetical order

    B. Have students pick a favorite letter in the alphabet

    C. Have students count the number of letters in their name

    D. Have students alphabetize the class names

24. **Before reading a story, what should students use to make predictions?**
    (Rigorous) (Skill 2.6)

    A. The first sentence in the book

    B. The cover and other illustrations in the story

    C. Information from other students

    D. The length of a book or story

25. **When should a KWL chart be filled out?**
    (Rigorous) (Skill 2.6)

    A. After reading only

    B. Before and during reading

    C. During reading only

    D. Before and after reading

26. In QAR (question answer relationship) a Right There question is one that: (Rigorous) (Skill 2.7)

   A. Requires the reader to combine their knowledge with information from the book

   B. Requires the reader to locate the information in one place in the book

   C. Requires the reader to locate information from several places in the book

   D. Requires the reader to draw only from their own experiences

27. If a teacher gives students a concept and asks students to formulate questions about that concept during reading and answer those questions after reading, what strategy is the teacher using? (Average) (Skill 2.7)

   A. Preview in Context

   B. Predicting

   C. Word Mapping

   D. Hierarchical and Linear Arrays

28. What is the best way to assess student's comprehension of reading material? (Average) (Skill 2.8)

   A. Have students read a page from the text aloud

   B. Have students write definitions of words using the dictionary

   C. Have students write a summary of what they have read

   D. Have students recommend a book to a classmate

29. Which choice shows the best way to check a student's comprehension of non-fiction reading selection is to: (Average) (Skill 2.7)

   A. Have the student point out the headings

   B. Have the student identify the main idea

   C. Have the student read all of the captions

   D. Have the student complete a vocabulary quiz

30. **What is the purpose of guide words in the dictionary?**
    (Easy) (Skill 2.9)

    A. They tell students the first and last word in that letter section

    B. They tell the definition of a word

    C. They are words that will guide students in how to spell a word

    D. They indicate the first and last word on a page in the dictionary

31. **What is one strategy students can use independently to understand written directions?**
    (Average) (Skill 2.10)

    A. Have someone read the directions aloud to the student

    B. Read the directions and highlight, or underline, key words

    C. Read only the beginning and ending of each paragraph

    D. Look at the samples given without reading the directions

MATH

1. **What is the product of 155 and 23?**
   (Average) (Skill 3.1)

   A. 3567

   B. 3565

   C. 465

   D. 775

2. **Which of the following is correct?**
   (Easy) (Skill 3.3)

   A. 2365 > 2340

   B. 0.75 > 1.25

   C. 3/4 < 1/16

   D. -5 < -6

3. **The difference between the product of 3 and 4 and the sum of 3 and 4 is**
   (Average) (Skill 3.4)

   A. 12

   B. 7

   C. -5

   D. 5

4. **The digit 8 in the number 975.086 is in the**
   (Easy) (Skill 3.5)

   A. Tenths place

   B. Ones place

   C. Hundredths place

   D. Hundreds place

5. **A coat is on sale for $135. If the discount offered is 25%, what was the original price of the coat?**
   (Rigorous) (Skill 3.6)

   A. $160

   B. $180

   C. $110

   D. $150

6. **Simplify:**

   $$\frac{5^{-2} \times 5^3}{5^5 \times 5^{-7}}$$

   (Average) (Skill 3.7)

   A. 5^5

   B. 125

   C. $\dfrac{1}{125}$

   D. 25

7. **Simplify:**

$$\frac{27 - 2.3^2}{8 \div 2^2 - (-2)^2}$$

(Rigorous) (Skill 3.8)

A. 9/2

B. 9/8

C. -4.5

D. 0.75

8. **At a publishing company, Mona can proofread 300 pages in 5 hours, while Lisa can proofread 360 pages in 4 hours. If they share the task of proofreading a 375-page document, how long will it take them to complete the job?** *(Rigorous) (Skill 3.10)*

A. 2.5 hours

B. 5 hours

C. 3 hours

D. 3.5 hours

9. **Solve for x:**

3(5 + 3x) – 8 = 88

(Average) (Skill 3.11)

A. 30

B. 9

C. 4.5

D. 27

10. **What is the next term in the sequence**

0.005, 0.03, 0.18, 1.08,...

(Rigorous) (Skill 3.12)

A. 1.96

B. 2.16

C. 3.32

D. 6.48

11. **The speed of light in space is about 3×10^8 meters per second. Express this in Kilometers per hour.** *(Average) (Skill 4.2)*

A. 1.08×10^9 Km / hr

B. 3.0×10^{11} Km / hr

C. 1.08×10^{12} Km / hr

D. 1.08×10^{15} Km / hr

12. **Which of the following shapes is not a parallelogram?**

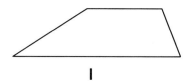

I

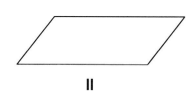

II

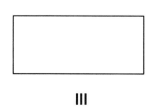

III

(Easy) (Skill 4.3)

A. I & III

B. II & III

C. I

D. I, II & III

13. **A cylinder-shaped container has a hemispherical top. If the radius of the container is r and the height of the cylindrical bottom is h, the total volume of the container and top is given by:**

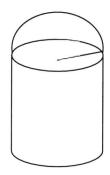

(Rigorous) (Skill 4.4)

A. $\pi r^2 h + 4\pi r^2$

B. $\pi r^2 h + \dfrac{4}{3}\pi r^3$

C. $\pi r^2 h + \dfrac{4}{3}\pi r^2$

D. $\pi r^2 h + \dfrac{2}{3}\pi r^3$

14. **The following set of points on a coordinate plane define an isosceles right triangle** *(Rigorous) (Skill 4.5)*

A. (4,0), (0,4), (4,4)

B. (4,0), (0,6), (4,4)

C. (0,0), (0,4), (5,2)

D. (0,0), (5,0), (5,2)

15. **What percentage of students got a C grade?**

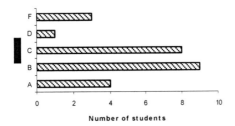

Number of students

(Average) (Skill 5.1)

A. 35

B. 8

C. 32

D. 40

16. **Which of the following is the most accurate inference that can be made from the graph shown below?**
(Average) (Skill 5.2)

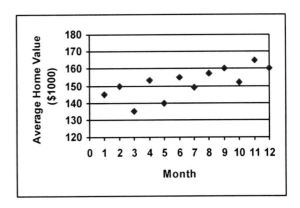

A. The average home value shows a decreasing trend over the 12-month period

B. The average home value shows an increasing trend over the 12-month period

C. The average home value stays about the same over the 12-month period

D. The data fluctuates too much to make any comment about the trend

17. You are creating a pie chart to show the expenses for a business. If employee pay is 40% of the total expenditure, what central angle will you use to show that segment of the pie chart?
(Average) (Skill 5.3)

 A. 72°

 B. 80°

 C. 40°

 D. 144°

18. Melissa scores 60, 68, and 75 in the first three of five tests. What should her average score be for the last two tests so that her mean test score for the 5 tests is 70?
(Rigorous) (Skill 5.4)

 A. 70

 B. 73.5

 C. 75.5

 D. 85

19. While doing the decimal division $50.5 \div 0.5$, a student gets the answer 1.01. The most likely explanation for this mistake is
(Average) (Competency 6)

 A. The student moved the decimal point to the left in the numerator but to the right in the denominator

 B. The student moved the decimal point to the right in the numerator but to the left in the denominator

 C. The student does not know how to do long division

 D. This was a careless mistake

20. A student performs the fraction multiplication $\frac{1}{2} \times \frac{1}{4} = \frac{1}{8}$ and is confused by the result. If multiplication is supposed to be repeated addition how is the result a smaller number? You can explain this anomaly by:
(Rigorous) (Competency 6)

 A. Drawing a diagram to illustrate fraction multiplication

 B. Pointing out that the repeated addition concept applies only to multiplication by whole numbers

 C. Explain multiplication as a scaling process

 D. All of the above

21. A paraprofessional uses the relationships shown below while explaining how to:

$$\frac{x}{100} = \frac{25}{40}; \quad \frac{30}{100} = \frac{x}{60}; \quad \frac{20}{100} = \frac{15}{x}$$

(Average) (Competency 6)

A. Solve proportion problems

B. Solve percentage problems

C. Do cross-multiplication

D. None of the above

22. A student performs the computation

$$\frac{2^5}{2^2} = 2^3 = 8$$

Which of the following exponent rules did she use? *(Easy) (Competency 6)*

A. $a^m \cdot a^n = a^{(m+n)}$

B. $\dfrac{a^m}{a^n} = a^{(m-n)}$

C. $\dfrac{a^{-m}}{a^{-n}} = \dfrac{a^n}{a^m}$

D. $a^0 = 1$

23. The common mnemonic used to remember the order of operations is: *(Easy) (Competency 6)*

A. PEDMAS

B. PEMDAS

C. MEPSAD

D. EMPADS

24. You are helping students list the steps needed to solve the word problem:
"Mr. Jones is 5 times as old as his son. Two years later he will be 4 times as old as his son. How old is Mr. Jones?"

One of the students makes the following list:

1. Assume Mr. Jones' son is x years old. Express Mr. Jones' age in terms of x.
2. Write how old they will be two years later in terms of x.
3. Solve the equation for x.
4. Multiply the answer by 5 to get Mr. Jones' age.

What step is missing between steps 2 and 3?
(Rigorous) (Competency 6)

A. Write an equation setting Mr. Jones age equal to 5 times his son's age

B. Write an equation setting Mr. Jones age two years later equal to 5 times his son's age two years later

C. Write an equation setting Mr. Jones age equal to 4 times his son's age

D. Write an equation setting Mr. Jones age two years later equal to 4 times his son's age two years later

25. The following equation is the best choice for teaching use of the distributive law in solving equations:
(Rigorous) (Competency 6)

A. $3(x + 5) = 4x$

B. $x(3 + 5) = 4$

C. $4(x + 2x) = 2$

D. None of the above

26. A student solves the following problem and gets an answer of 45. What is the most likely reason for her mistake?

"Sara left for school at quarter to ten and reached there at half past ten. How many hours did it take her to travel to school?"

(Easy) (Competency 6)

A. She does not know what "quarter to" means

B. She does not know what "half past" means

C. She did not notice that the problem asks for the answer in hours

D. She does not know that there are 60 minutes in an hour

27. **A student does not know how to begin finding the area of the following shape:**

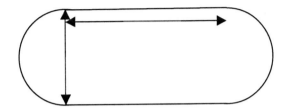

How can a paraprofessional help him to get started?
(Average) (Competency 6)

A. Ask him to divide the area into a rectangle and two half circles

B. Tell him to compute
$$1.5 \times 3 + \pi(0.75)^2$$

C. Ask him whether the shape can be divided into familiar shapes such as rectangles, squares, triangles, and circles

D. Tell him the formula for the area of a rectangle and the area of a circle

28. **You are helping a group of students identify which of several triangles drawn on a coordinate plane are right triangles. If the coordinates of the vertices are given, the students can identify the right triangles if:**
(Rigorous) (Competency 6)

A. They know only the Pythagorean theorem and the distance formula

B. They know only the slope formula and the relationship between the slopes of perpendicular lines

C. They don't know any of the formulae mentioned in A and B but the legs of the right triangle are parallel to the x and y axes

D. All of the above

29. A student is creating a circle graph. Which of these skills is it absolutely necessary for her to have in order to do the task?

   A. Determining the central angle for a sector of the circle

   B. Finding the area of the sector of a circle

   C. Computing percentages

(Rigorous) (Competency 6)

   A. A only

   B. A and B

   C. A and C

   D. C only

30. A student was asked to find the median of the set of numbers

"1, 14, 2, 6, 27, 9, 7, 11, 23"

He came up with the answer "27." What was the likely cause of his error?
(Average) (Competency 6)

   A. He did not know what median means and picked a random number

   B. He did not put the numbers in order before identifying the middle number

   C. He picked the largest number

   D. He added up the 3 middle numbers

WRITING

Directions: Read the following passage and answer question 1.

Ants have three main parts to their bodies. The first part is the head, which contains the jaw, eyes, and antennae. The second part of an ant's body is the trunk. The trunk has six legs attached to it. The third part of an ant's body is the rear. I was surprised to learn that the rear contains a poison sac. This is one way the ant defends itself.

1. **What type of writing is demonstrated in the passage above?**
    (Rigorous) (Skill 1.7)

    A. Descriptive

    B. Narrative

    C. Expository

    D. Persuasive

2. **What is the plural of the word _rose_?**
    (Easy) (Skill 1.8)

    A. Rosis

    B. Rosses

    C. Roses

    D. Rose's

3. **Which word needs to be corrected in the sentence below?**
    (Rigorous) (Skill 1.8)

    The presents on the table is wrapped in beautiful wrapping paper.

    A. presents

    B. is

    C. wrapped

    D. beautiful

4. **Which sentence is punctuated correctly?**
    (Easy) (Skill 1.8)

    A. The dog escaped from the house this morning.

    B. What time will you be home tonight?

    C. The coffee is very hot!

    D. I haven't had lunch yet?

5. **What type of sentence is the sentence below?**
(Rigorous) (Skill 1.8)

Jarrett and Austin like to read and write.

A. Simple

B. Compound

C. Complex

D. Compound/complex

6. **What must be done to make this sentence correct?**
(Rigorous) (Skill 1.8)

Before the children were allowed to go outside.

A. Place a comma after *before*

B. Change the word *children* to *child*

C. Change the period to a comma and add an independent clause

D. Nothing, it is fine the way it is

7. **When students just sit down and write about a topic, writing everything that comes to mind, this is called:**
(Average) (Skill 2.6)

A. Brainstorming

B. Outlining

C. Free writing

D. Drafting

8. **What is the difference between drafting and revising?**
(Rigorous) (Skill 2.6)

A. Nothing, they are the same thing

B. Drafting is the first copy, and revising is the final copy

C. Drafting is the first copy and revising corrects spelling errors etc.

D. Drafting is the first copy, and revising improves the craft of writing

9. **What is the purpose of editing?**
   (Average) (Skill 2.6)

   A. To publish a piece of writing for presentation

   B. To rewrite it in one's neatest handwriting

   C. To spell check-it in a word processing program

   D. To check it for spelling, correct punctuation, and grammar

10. **Students in a classroom are asked to keep a Writer's Notebook that they write in every day. What is the purpose of this notebook?**
    (Rigorous) (Skill 3.6)

    A. To write down ideas for poems that students might want to write

    B. To keep lists of ideas on certain topics that might be developed later

    C. To draw quick sketches and then write about them in greater detail

    D All of the above

11. **Which word best completes the sentence?**
    (Easy) (Skill 7.1)

    Maria lost two _____ when she was in kindergarten.

    A. teeth

    B. tooth

    C. tooths

    D. toothes

12. **Which word will complete the sentence?**
    (Average) (Skill 7.2)

    The Johnson's painted _____ house a beautiful shade of yellow.

    A. they're

    B. their

    C. there

    D. them

13. **Which word will complete the sentence?**
    (Average) (Skill 7.2)

    We waited _____ long in the movie line.

    A. too

    B. to

    C. two

    D. tow

14. Jessica asked her brother what time dinner would be ready. He responded by saying, "I could care less." Is Jessica's brother's response correct?
(Easy) (Skill 7.2)

A. Yes

B. No

15. Which word will complete the sentence?
(Rigorous) (Skill 7.3)

That _____ wings are yellow and black.

A. butterfly's

B. butterflys'

C. butterflies

D. butterflie's

16. Which sentence is correct?
(Rigorous) (Skill 7.3)

A. Birds scurrying by to find food in the snow.

B. Birds scurry by to find food in the snow.

C. Birds, scurry by to find food in the snow.

D. Birds scurry by, to find, food in the snow.

17. Which punctuation mark is required, if any, in the sentence?
(Easy) (Skill 7.3)

I won't wear plaid stripes, and checks together.

A. !

B. ?

C. ,

D. None

18. What type of sentence is the sentence below?
(Average) (Skill 7.4)

I was late for the movies but I got popcorn anyway.

A. Simple

B. Compound

C. Complex

D. Compound/complex

19. **Which sentence is a run-on sentence?**
(Rigorous) (Skill 7.4)

A. It was Jill's first day at her new school and she was eager to make friends.

B. During lunch Jill sat down at a table Jill ate her sandwich and drank her milk.

C. Before long a girl came up and asked Jill if she could sit with her.

D. As soon as they began talking Jill knew they would become friends.

20. **Which change, if any, would make the underlined words correct?**
(Easy) (Skill 7.5)

I'm sorry that I haven't wrote to you in such a long time.

A. haven't written

B. haven't writed

C. didn't written

D. No change necessary

21. **Which change, if any, would make the underlined word correct?**
(Rigorous) (Skill 7.5)

There are so many characteristics that I like about her, especially the way she cares about the feelings of others and give them her love and devotion.

A. gave

B. gives

C. given

D. No change necessary

22. **Which word will make the sentence correct?**
(Easy) (Skill 7.5)

On your way home from work tonight, please stop at the store and pick up some milk, two _____ of bread, and some vegetables for salad.

A. loafs

B. loafes

C. loaves

D. loavs

23. **Which sentence is written correctly?**
(Easy) (Skill 7.5)

   A. We watched the game, then get tired and gone home.

   B. We watch the game, then got tired and go home.

   C. We watched the game, then got tired and went home.

   D. We watched the game, then get tired and goes home.

24. **Which word will correctly complete the sentence?**
(Average) (Skill 7.5)

   _____ tails range from breed to breed. Some are very short and curly while others are long and straight.

   A. Dogs

   B. Dogs'

   C. Dog's

   D. Doges

Directions: Choose the correctly spelled word to complete each sentence for questions 25 to 29.

25. **I _____ forget to lock my front door before I leave the house in the morning.**
(Average) (Skill 7.6)

   A. occasionaly

   B. occasionally

26. **Don't purchase that vehicle unless they offer you a money back _____.**
(Average) (Skill 7.6)

   A. guaruntee

   B. guarantee

27. **A prior _____ will cause us to be late to the celebration.**
(Average) (Skill 7.6)

   A. committment

   B. commitment

28. **It is quite an _____ to graduate from high school and continue on to college.**
(Average) (Skill 7.6)

   A. achievement

   B. acheivement

29. Due to _____ weather, all after school activities will be cancelled today.
(Average) (Skill 7.6)

A. inclement

B. inclemet

30. Before students write a personal narrative, what ideas should be part of their prewriting?
(Rigorous) (Skill 8.1)

A Characters, setting, problem, solution

B The beginning and the ending

C How the piece will be organized; for example, a circle story

D Sequence of events

31. If you are helping a student locate information about their state for a research report, what other source can be used besides the Internet?
(Rigorous) (Skill 8.2)

A. A dictionary

B. An atlas

C. An almanac

D. A thesaurus

32. When students are writing, which reference book should students use to find synonyms for weak nouns, verbs, and adjectives?
(Rigorous) (Skill 8.2)

A. A dictionary

B. An encyclopedia

C. An atlas

D. A thesaurus

33. What is another name for a "thesis statement"?
(Average) (Skill 8.3)

A. A main idea sentence

B. An introductory paragraph

C. A concluding sentence

D. A hook

34. How is a five-paragraph essay typically organized?
(Average) (Skill 8.3)

A. Thesis statement, body, ending thesis

B. Introduction, body, conclusion

C. Introduction, thesis, conclusion

D. Thesis, introduction, conclusion

35. What is the purpose of a topic sentence in the body paragraphs of an essay? *(Average) (Skill 8.3)*

A. It states the main idea of the paragraph it begins

B. It restates the thesis statement in another way

C. It supports an opposing point of view

D. It asks a question for the reader to consider

36. What is a good way to edit a paper if it has been handwritten? *(Rigorous) (Skill 8.4)*

A. Read the paper backwards

B. Have a peer review your paper

C. Read the paper aloud

D. All of the above

37. What are the three reasons that authors write? *(Average) (Skill 8.5)*

A To be graded, to be published, they have to

B To entertain, to inform, to persuade

C To remind, to show, to tell

D To be heard, to be seen, to be noticed

38. How does the audience of the piece effect how it is written? *(Rigorous) (Skill 8.5)*

A. The audience of a piece does not effect how a piece is written

B. It will determine how long the writing has to be

C. The audience will review the writing and give it a grade

D. It will determine the language used in the piece

39. What type of writing has a sequence of events that recounts an event? *(Average) (Skill 8.6)*

A. Persuasive

B. Descriptive

C. Narrative

D. Letter

40. **If a students wants to write to the principal in an attempt to have the principal change a school rule, which type of writing will the student most likely produce?**
(Rigorous) (Skill 8.6)

A. Narrative

B. Descriptive

C. Persuasive

D. Expository

READING

Directions: Read the following passage and answer questions 1-3.

Oberlin, Ohio, is located south of Lake Eerie and about 40 miles east of Toledo, Ohio. Oberlin, Ohio, is home to about 8,000 residents who find it to be a lovely place to call home. It is also home to Oberlin College. Oberlin College is a private liberal arts school that was established on September 2, 1833. Oberlin is home to approximately 2,850 students and 1,058 staff members. Perhaps it is most notably known for being the first college in the United States to regularly admit African-American students in 1835. In 1837, Oberlin College became one of the first co-educational colleges when it admitted four women, Mary Kellogg, Mary Caroline Rudd, Mary Hosfor, and Elizabeth Prall. Consequently, in 1841 it was one of the first colleges to confer degrees on women when they graduated four years later.

1. **What is the main idea of the above passage?**
   (Average) (Skill 1.1)

   A.   Oberlin, Ohio, is a lovely place to live

   B.   Oberlin College is a private liberal arts school

   C.   Oberlin College is well known for its many firsts

   D.   Oberlin College was one of the first schools to grant degrees to women

Answer: C. Oberlin College is well known for its many firsts
Choice A is an opinion that is presented in the passage. Choices A and D are details about Oberlin College.

2. **What is the author's purpose?**
    (Rigorous) (Skill 1.1)

    A.   To inform

    B.   To entertain

    C.   To describe

    D.   To narrate

Answer: A. To inform
The author is offering information about Oberlin College. Although some people might find the passage entertaining, this is not the best answer. This is also true of choice C. The author does not really describe Oberlin College, but does inform the reader of its history.

3. **Which detail supports the idea that Oberlin College was a pioneer in the area of equal rights for women?**
    (Rigorous) (Skill 1.3)

    A.   Oberlin college became one of the first co-educational colleges when it admitted four women

    B.   Mary Kellogg attended Oberlin college

    C.   Mary Hosfor received a degree from Oberlin College in 1841

    D.   Oberlin College began to regularly admit African-Americans in 1835

Answer: A. Oberlin college became one of the first co-educational colleges when it admitted four women
Pioneer means the first to do something. Choice A supports this idea.

Directions: Read the following passage and answer questions 4.

Many people say that the story *The Ugly Duckling* mirrors Hans Christian Andersen's childhood. He was an odd child and did not fit in well with other children. Hans was often older than other children and because of this felt alienated. He was interested in the stage and visited the playhouse outside of Copenhagen with his father. However, eventually he was sent away to a boarding school. His experience there was dreadful. He lived with the schoolmaster where he was abused. The headmaster had said it was a way to improve his character.

4. **Which detail supports the main idea, "Hans Christian Andersen had a difficult childhood"?**
    (Rigorous) (Skill 1.2)

    A.   Hans Christian Andersen's headmaster abused him

    B.   Hans' life mirrored that of *The Ugly Duckling*

    C.   Hans was often older than other children

    D.   Hans enjoyed the theatre as a child

Answer: A. Hans Christian Andersen's headmaster abused him
B draws a comparison between one of his stories and his childhood. Choices C and D are details, but they do not support the main idea that Andersen had a difficult childhood.

5. **A student writes an essay that shows the similarities and differences between a book and a movie of the same title. What type of essay is it?**
    (Easy) (Skill 1.3)

    A.   Classification

    B.   Compare and contrast

    C.   Cause and effect

    D.   Statement support

Answer: B. Compare and contrast
The student's essay compares and contrasts the book and the movie of the same title.

6. **In Writer's Workshop students are asked to write a personal narrative. How should their writing be organized?**
   (Average) (Skill 1.3)

   A.　　Statement support

   B.　　Compare and contrast

   C.　　Sequence of events

   D.　　Classification

Answer: C. Sequence of events
A narrative is a retelling of events in order.

7. **Engineers thought it would be difficult to *construct* the Golden Gate Bridge because of the weather conditions and the ocean currents that exist in California.**
   (Easy) (Skill 1.4)

   What does the word *construct* mean in the sentence above?

   A.　　Drive across

   B.　　Close down

   C.　　Make longer

   D.　　Build or create

Answer: D. Build or create
Engineers are people that build or create things. They thought it would be hard to do that because the weather and the water currents in San Francisco made the job challenging.

8. **If you have had a cough for a long time, it is said to be:**
(Rigorous) (Skill 1.4)

    A.   Chronic

    B.   Prescriptive

    C.   Contagious

    D.   Malicious

Answer: A. Chronic
The root –chrono- means *time.* Chronic therefore means "a long time".

Directions: Read the following passage and answer questions 9.

Time seemed to be passing so slowly. Leslie looked at the clock for at least the hundredth time in the past hour. She turned back and looked the other way. Soon this became uncomfortable too and she turned and laid on her back. This position also didn't feel right so she turned back toward the clock. Twenty minutes had passed. "Umph," Leslie grunted closing her eyes again.

9. **From Leslie's actions we can determine that**
(Average) (Skill 1.5)

    A.   Leslie is laying on the beach somewhere

    B.   Leslie is at the doctor's office waiting her turn

    C.   Leslie is excited about an upcoming event

    D.   Leslie is having a difficult time sleeping

Answer: D. Leslie is having a difficult time sleeping
The clock, trying to find a satisfying position, the frustration—these are all clues that Leslie is having a hard time sleeping.

Directions: Read the following passage and answer questions 10.

Molly slid into her gorgeous dress. She had imagined this day since she was a young girl living in Hartford, Connecticut. Checking herself in the mirror one last time, she decided that this was as good as it was going to get. Her hair was perfect, just the way she had imagined—the hairdresser had definitely earned her fee this morning. As did the make-up specialist Molly thought to herself as she examined her face in the mirror. Then she heard the anthem of the orchestra. She turned from the mirror and headed toward the aisle.

10. **It can be inferred from the passage above that Molly is:**
    (Average) (Skill 1.5)

    A.   A runway model

    B.   About to get married

    C.   Shopping at a store

    D.   A Broadway performer

Answer: B. About to get married
The clues that allow us to decide that Molly is about to get married because she puts on a gorgeous dress, has imagined this day since she was young, and had her hair and her make-up done. She then hears the orchestra begin to play, and she heads toward the aisle.

11. **All of the following statements are opinions EXCEPT**
    (Average) (Skill 1.6)

    A.   Mrs. Krissy is the best teacher at Ringdale Elementary School

    B.   The third grade test is difficult for the students

    C.   Ringdale Elementary School hasn't been around that long

    D.   There are 853 students at Ringdale Elementary School

Answer: D. There are 853 students at Ringdale Elementary School
D is the correct answer because it is the only statement that can be verified.

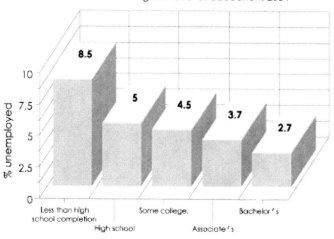

Unemployment rates of persons 25 years old and over, by highest level of education: 2004

U.S. Department of Labor, Bureau of Labor Statistics, Office of Employment and Unemployment Statistics. Current Population Survey (CPS), 2004.

12. **According to the graph, what group of people made up the largest percentage of the unemployed in 2004?**
   (Average) (Skill 1.7)

   A.   Those who did not complete High School

   B.   Those who completed High School

   C.   Those who have taken some college credit

   D.   Those who possess a Bachelor's degree

Answer: A. Those who did not complete High School
The tallest bar equals 8.5%. The x-axis represents the highest level of education completed and the y-axis represents the % unemployed.

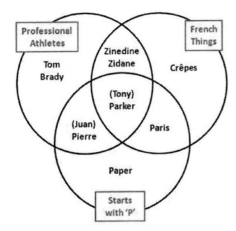

Sample Venn Diagram

13. According to the Venn Diagram, what is true about "Paris"?
(Rigorous) (Skill 1.7)

    A.   It starts with "P"

    B.   It is a French Thing

    C.   It is the name of a professional athlete

    D.   It starts with "P" and is a French Thing

Answer: D. It starts with "P" and is a French Thing
The Venn Diagram has three categories represented by three different circles. Paris is in two circles; French Things and Starts with "P".

14. According to the Venn Diagram, what fits within all three categories?
(Rigorous) (Skill 1.7)

    A.   Tony Parker

    B.   Zinedine Zidane

    C.   Juan Pierre

    D.   Paris

Answer: A. Tony Parker
Tony Parker is in the middle of three overlapping circles and therefore, meets all three criteria: French Things, Professional Athletes; Starts with "P".

15. A student is reading and gets stuck on the word *sure.* All of the following are good ways to help the student decode the word EXCEPT *(Average) (Skill 2.1)*

    A.   Have the student sound it out

    B.   Have the student skip the word and come back

    C.   Tell the student is rhymes with *lure*

    D.   Tell the student that *ur* makes the *er* sound

Answer: A. Have the student sound it out
Sounding out the word won't work for this particular word because normally /sh/ makes the "sh" sound, and u-e normally makes a long /e/ sound.

16. How many syllables does the word *chocolate* have? *(Easy) (Skill 2.1)*

    A.   1

    B.   2

    C.   3

    D.   4

Answer: C. 3
Although we may pronounce *chocolate* using two syllables, it technically has 3: *choc-o-late.*

17. **How does adding the prefix *dis-* to the word *continue*, change its meaning?**
(Average) (Skill 2.2)

    A.   It now means "to continue later"

    B.   It now means "to do again"

    C.   It now means "to not continue"

    D.   It doesn't change the meaning

Answer: C. It now means "to not continue"
The prefix *dis-* means *not*. Therefore, the meaning of the word *discontinue* means to "not continue."

18. **Which combination of words produces an irregular contraction?**
(Average) (Skill 2.2)

    A.   did + not

    B.   you + are

    C.   I + will

    D.   will + not

Answer: D. will + not
The contraction for will + not is won't. Choices A, B, and C are all regular combinations where the first word doesn't change when making the contraction: didn't, you're, I'll.

19. **Besides teaching scientific methods and information, what might be a good lesson to teach along with a book about photosynthesis?**
(Rigorous) (Skill 2.2)

    A.   The first photograph taken

    B.   The root –photo- means light

    C.   The food chain

    D.   The letter /ph/ make the "f" sound

Answer: B. The root –photo- means light
Although all lessons would be a good extension of what photosynthesis is, the best answer is B, teaching students Latin and Greek roots when it is connected with meaning and prior knowledge.

20. **A student reads the sentence, "The boy saw a worm in the ground," and says "The boy saw a worm in the grass." What might you say to the student as a paraprofessional?**
(Rigorous) (Skill 2.3)

    A.   "You said grass. Look at this word and tell me why it can't be grass."

    B.   "Look at this word again [pointing to ground]. What sound does this word begin with?

    C.   "What vowels do you see in this word? [pointing to ground]"

    D.   "Where is another place you might see a worm?"

Answer: A. "You said grass. Look at this word and tell me why it can't be grass."
Although D is another good thing to ask the student, A is better. This option draws the student's attention to the word "ground" and makes them analyze the letter-sound relationship.

21. **What is a synonym for the word "fast"?**
    (Easy) (Skill 2.4)

    A.   Slow

    B.   Last

    C.   Speedy

    D.   Quickly

Answer: C. Speedy
A synonym is a word that has the same meaning. Fast and speedy are interchangeable and mean the same thing. Choice A is an antonym, or opposite, of fast. B simply rhymes with fast. D doesn't work because it is an adverb and *fast* is an adjective.

22. **Which word belongs in the blank?**
    (Easy) (Skill 2.4)

    Some people like to paint _____ houses garish colors.

    A.   they're

    B.   there

    C.   their

    D.   None of these work

Answer: C. their
The word *their* shows ownership of something. The house belongs to the people. Therefore, *their* is the correct word. *There* is a place; *they're* is a contraction for the words they + are.

23. What is the best strategy to help students alphabetize words? (Rigorous) (Skill 2.5)

    A.   Have students write random words in alphabetical order

    B.   Have students pick a favorite letter in the alphabet

    C.   Have students count the number of letters in their name

    D.   Have students alphabetize the class names

Answer: D. Have students alphabetize the class names
Students need to use meaningful information in their learning. At a young age, students are interested in their names and the names of their classmates. Counting the number of letters in their name (Choice C) is a great math activity and will help students with their alphabetizing.

24. Before reading a story, what should students use to make predictions? (Rigorous) (Skill 2.6)

    A.   The first sentence in the book

    B.   The cover and other illustrations in the story

    C.   Information from other students

    D.   The length of a book or story

Answer: B. The cover and other illustrations in the story
Students need to get their minds ready to read and therefore must do a picture walk through a book looking at the cover illustration and other illustrations in the story.

25. When should a KWL chart be filled out?
(Rigorous) (Skill 2.6)

    A.   After reading only

    B.   Before and during reading

    C.   During reading only

    D.   Before and after reading

Answer: D. Before and after reading
The K stands for "What we KNOW," the W stands for "What we WANT to know," and L stands for "What we want to LEARN." A KWL chart is filled in before reading and after reading. It may also be completed during reading to monitor reading.

26. In QAR (question answer relationship) a Right There question is one that:
(Rigorous) (Skill 2.7)

    A.   Requires the reader to combine their knowledge with information from the book.

    B.   Requires the reader to locate the information in one place in the book.

    C.   Requires the reader to locate information from several places in the book.

    D.   Requires the reader to draw only from their own experiences.

Answer: B. Requires the reader to locate the information in one place in the book.
In QAR, there are four types of questions: Right There, Think and Search, Author and Me, and On My Own. A Right There question requires the reader to find the answer in on particular place in the story.

27. **If a teacher gives students a concept and asks students to formulate questions about that concept during reading and answer those questions after reading, what strategy is the teacher using?**
   (Average) (Skill 2.7)

   A.   Preview in Context

   B.   Predicting

   C.   Word Mapping

   D.   Hierarchical and Linear Arrays

Answer: C. Word Mapping
When students preview in context, students are taught vocabulary directly prior to reading. Choice B, predicting, is a reading strategy, but students predict before and during reading. A word map, Choice C, is when students are given a theme idea and ask questions about it and answer those questions during reading. In heirarchical and linear arrays, students rank vocabulary words.

28. **What is the best way to assess student's comprehension of reading material?**
   (Average) (Skill 2.8)

   A.   Have students read a page from the text aloud

   B.   Have students write definitions of words using the dictionary

   C.   Have students write a summary of what they have read

   D.   Have students recommend a book to a classmate

Answer: C. Have students write a summary of what they have read
A summary will check the comprehension of students to see if they understood the characters and their problem, the major events in the plot, and the resolution.

29. **Which choice shows the best way to check a student's comprehension of non-fiction reading selection is to:**
   (Average) (Skill 2.7)

   A.   Have the student point out the headings

   B.   Have the student identify the main idea

   C.   Have the student read all of the captions

   D.   Have the student complete a vocabulary quiz

Answer: B. Have the student identify the main idea
If a student can identify the main idea of a non-fiction reading selection, then they are showing that they were able to comprehend the text. Students should preview headings and captions (Choice A and C) before reading. Vocabulary should always be taught authentically; therefore Choice D is not the best answer.

30. **What is the purpose of guide words in the dictionary?**
   (Easy) (Skill 2.9)

   A.   They tell students the first and last word in that letter section

   B.   They tell the definition of a word

   C.   They are words that will guide students in how to spell a word

   D.   They indicate the first and last word on a page in the dictionary

Answer: D. They indicate the first and last word on a page in the dictionary
Guide words are the words on the top of each dictionary page. There is one on the left of the page and one on the right. This lets students know what the first word on that page is and what the last word is.

31. **What is one strategy students can use independently to understand written directions?**
(Average) (Skill 2.10)

    A.   Have someone read the directions aloud to the student

    B.   Read the directions and highlight, or underline, key words

    C.   Read only the beginning and ending of each paragraph

    D.   Look at the samples given without reading the directions

Answer: B. Read the directions and highlight, or underline, key words
Choice B is the best answer. Students should be taught how to use highlighters effectively.

Answer Key: Reading

1.	C
2.	A
3.	A
4.	A
5.	B
6.	C
7.	D
8.	A
9.	D
10.	B
11.	D
12.	A
13.	D
14.	A
15.	A
16.	C
17.	C
18.	D
19.	B
20.	A
21.	C
22.	C
23.	D
24.	B
25.	D
26.	B
27.	C
28.	C
29.	B
30.	D
31.	B

Rigor Table: Reading

	Easy 20%	Average 40%	Rigorous 40%
Questions	5, 7, 16, 21, 22, 30,	1, 6, 9,10, 11, 12, 15, 17, 18, 27, 28, 29	2, 3, 4, 8, 13, 14, 19, 20, 23, 24, 25, 26

MATH

1. **What is the product of 155 and 23?**
    (Average) (Skill 3.1)

    A.   3567
    B.   3565
    C.   465
    D.   775

Answer: B. 3565

$$
\begin{array}{r}
155 \\
\times\ 23 \\
\hline
465 \\
3100 \\
\hline
3565
\end{array}
$$

2. **Which of the following is   correct?**
    (Easy) (Skill 3.3)

    A. $2365 > 2340$

    B. $0.75 > 1.25$

    C. $3/4 \ < 1/16$

    D. $-5 < -6$

Answer is A. 2365 > 2340

3. The difference between the product of 3 and 4 and the sum of 3 and 4 is:
(Average) (Skill 3.4)

   A.   12

   B.   7

   C.   -5

   D.   5

Answer: D. 5
The product of 3 and 4 is 12. The sum of 3 and 4 is 7. The difference between them is 12 – 7 = 5.

4. The digit 8 in the number 975.086 is in the
(Easy) (Skill 3.5)

   A.   Tenths place

   B.   Ones place

   C.   Hundredths place

   D.   Hundreds place

Answer is C. Hundredths place

5. **A coat is on sale for \$135. If the discount offered is 25%, what was the original price of the coat?**
(Rigorous) (Skill 3.6)

    A.   \$160

    B.   \$180

    C.   \$110

    D.   \$150

Answer: B. \$180
Since the discount is 25%, the sale price \$135 is 75% of the original price. Hence

$$\frac{135}{75} \times \frac{100}{1} = \frac{540}{3} = \$180$$

6. **Simplify:**

$$\frac{5^{-2} \times 5^3}{5^5 \times 5^{-7}}$$

(Average) (Skill 3.7)

    A. 5^5

    B.   125

    C. $\dfrac{1}{125}$

    D.   25

Answer: B. 125

$$\frac{5^{-2} \times 5^3}{5^5 \times 5^{-7}} = \frac{5^{-2+3}}{5^{5-7}} = \frac{5}{5^{-2}} = 5^{1+2} = 5^3 = 125$$

7. **Simplify:**

$$\frac{27 - 2.3^2}{8 \div 2^2 - (-2)^2}$$

(Rigorous) (Skill 3.8)

    A.   9/2

    B.   9/8

    C.   -4.5

    D.   0.75

Answer: C. -4.5

$$\frac{27 - 2.3^2}{8 \div 2^2 - (-2)^2} = \frac{27 - 18}{2 - 4} = -\frac{9}{2} = -4.5$$

8. **At a publishing company, Mona can proofread 300 pages in 5 hours, while Lisa can proofread 360 pages in 4 hours. If they share the task of proofreading a 375-page document, how long will it take them to complete the job?**
(Rigorous) (Skill 3.10)

    A.   2.5 hours

    B.   5 hours

    C.   3 hours

    D.   3.5 hours

Answer: A. 2.5 hours
Since Mona proofreads 300/5 = 60 pages in one hour and Lisa proofreads 360/4 = 90 pages in one hour, together they can proofread 90 + 60 = 150 pages per hour. Hence it would take then 375/150 = 2.5 hours to complete the job.

9.   Solve for x:

3(5 + 3x) – 8 = 88

(Average) (Skill 3.11)

A.   30

B.   9

C.   4.5

D.   27

Answer: B. 9
3(5 + 3x) – 8 = 88;   15 + 9x – 8 = 88;   7 + 9x = 88;   9x = 81;   x = 9

10. What is the next term in the sequence

0.005, 0.03, 0.18, 1.08,…

(Rigorous) (Skill 3.12)

A.   1.96

B.   2.16

C.   3.32

D.   6.48

Answer: D. 6.48
This is a geometric sequence where each term is obtained by multiplying the preceding term by the common ration 6. Thus, the next term in the sequence is 1.08 x 6 = 6.48.

11. **The speed of light in space is about** 3×10^8 **meters per second. Express this in Kilometers per hour.**
(Average) (Skill 4.2)

    A. $1.08 \times 10^9 \, Km/hr$

    B. $3.0 \times 10^{11} \, Km/hr$

    C. $1.08 \times 10^{12} \, Km/hr$

    D. $1.08 \times 10^{15} \, Km/hr$

Answer: A. $1.08 \times 10^9 \, Km/hr$

$$3 \times 10^8 \, \frac{m}{s} = 3 \times 10^8 \, \frac{m}{s} \times \frac{1Km}{1000m} \times \frac{3600s}{1\,hr} = 108 \times 10^7 \, \frac{Km}{hr} = 1.08 \times 10^9 \, \frac{Km}{hr}$$

12. Which of the following shapes is not a parallelogram?

I

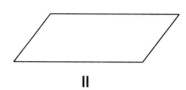

II

III

(Easy) (Skill 4.3)

A.   I & III

B.   II & III

C.   I

D.   I, II & III

Answer is C. I
A parallelogram is a quadrilateral with two pairs of parallel sides.

13. **A cylinder-shaped container has a hemispherical top. If the radius of the container is r and the height of the cylindrical bottom is h, the total volume of the container and top is given by**

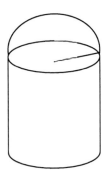

(Rigorous) (Skill 4.4)

A. $\pi r^2 h + 4\pi r^2$

B. $\pi r^2 h + \dfrac{4}{3}\pi r^3$

C. $\pi r^2 h + \dfrac{4}{3}\pi r^2$

D. $\pi r^2 h + \dfrac{2}{3}\pi r^3$

Answer: D. $\pi r^2 h + \dfrac{2}{3}\pi r^3$

Note that the volume of a sphere of radius r is $\dfrac{4}{3}\pi r^3$. Since the top is half of a sphere, its volume will be half that of a sphere of radius r.

14. **The following set of points on a coordinate plane define an isosceles right triangle**
    (Rigorous) (Skill 4.5)

    A.   (4,0), (0,4), (4,4)

    B.   (4,0), (0,6), (4,4)

    C.   (0,0), (0,4), (5,2)

    D.   (0,0), (5.0), (5,2)

Answer is A. (4,0), (0,4), (4,4)
Choice D defines a right triangle that is not isosceles, choice C defines an isosceles triangle that is not right, and choice B defines a triangle that is neither isosceles nor right.

15. **What percentage of students got a C grade?**

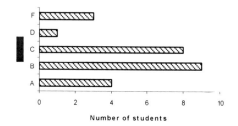

    (Average) (Skill 5.1)

    A.   35

    B.   8

    C.   32

    D.   40

Answer: C. 32
The total number of students = 4 + 9 + 8 + 1 + 3 = 25.
The number of students who got C = 8.
Hence, the percentage of students that got C = (8/25)x100= 32.

16. **Which of the following is the most accurate inference that can be made from the graph shown below?**
(Average) (Skill 5.2)

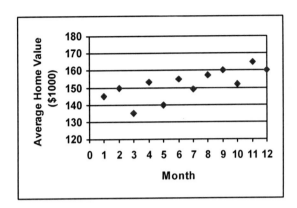

A.   The average home value shows a decreasing trend over the 12-month period

B.   The average home value shows an increasing trend over the 12-month period

C.   The average home value stays about the same over the 12-month period

D.   The data fluctuates too much to make any comment about the trend

Answer is B. The average home value shows an increasing trend over the 12-month period
Even though the data fluctuates, it shows an unmistakable upward trend towards the right.

17. You are creating a pie chart to show the expenses for a business. If employee pay is 40% of the total expenditure, what central angle will you use to show that segment of the pie chart?
(Average) (Skill 5.3)

    A. $72°$

    B. $80°$

    C. $40°$

    D. $144°$

Answer is D. $144°$
Since employee pay is 40% of the total, the central angle will be 40% of $360°$ = $(40/100) \times 360° = 144°$.

18. Melissa scores 60, 68, and 75 in the first three of five tests. What should her average score be for the last two tests so that her mean test score for the 5 tests is 70?
(Rigorous) (Skill 5.4)

    A.   70

    B.   73.5

    C.   75.5

    D.   85

Answer: B. 73.5
Let Melissa's average score for the last two tests be x. Then,
$60 + 68 + 75 + 2x = 70 \times 5$
$2x = 350 - 203 = 147$
$x = 73.5$

19. **While doing the decimal division** $50.5 \div 0.5$, **a student gets the answer 1.01. The most likely explanation for this mistake is**
    (Average) (Competency 6)

> A.   The student moved the decimal point to the left in the numerator but to the right in the denominator

> B.   The student moved the decimal point to the right in the numerator but to the left in the denominator

> C.   The student does not know how to do long division

> D.   This was a careless mistake

Answer: A. The student moved the decimal point to the left in the numerator but to the right in the denominator
The student moved the decimal point to the left in the numerator but to the right in the denominator. Hence he did $50.5 \div 0.5 = 5.05 \div 5.0 = 1.01$.

20. **A student performs the fraction multiplication** $\dfrac{1}{2} \times \dfrac{1}{4} = \dfrac{1}{8}$ **and is confused by the result. If multiplication is supposed to be repeated addition how is the result a smaller number? You can explain this anomaly by:**
    (Rigorous) (Competency 6)

> A.   Drawing a diagram to illustrate fraction multiplication

> B.   Pointing out that the repeated addition concept applies only to multiplication by whole numbers

> C.   Explain multiplication as a scaling process

> D.   All of the above

Answer: D. All of the above
The idea of scaling expressed by drawing diagrams for both whole numbers and fractions would be the best way to explain multiplication.

21. **A paraprofessional uses the relationships shown below while explaining how to**

$$\frac{x}{100} = \frac{25}{40}; \quad \frac{30}{100} = \frac{x}{60}; \quad \frac{20}{100} = \frac{15}{x}$$

(Average) (Competency 6)

A.   Solve proportion problems

B.   Solve percentage problems

C.   Do cross-multiplication

D.   None of the above

Answer: B. Solve percentage problems
The relationships do involve proportions as well as cross-multiplication. However, in each case one denominator is always 100. Thus, these obviously relate to percentage problems.

22. **A student performs the computation**

$$\frac{2^5}{2^2} = 2^3 = 8$$

Which of the following exponent rules did she use?
(Easy) (Competency 6)

A. $a^m \cdot a^n = a^{(m+n)}$

B. $\dfrac{a^m}{a^n} = a^{(m-n)}$

C. $\dfrac{a^{-m}}{a^{-n}} = \dfrac{a^n}{a^m}$

D. $a^0 = 1$

Answer: B. $\dfrac{a^m}{a^n} = a^{(m-n)}$

23. The common mnemonic used to remember the order of operations is: (Easy) (Competency 6)

   A.   PEDMAS

   B.   PEMDAS

   C.   MEPSAD

   D.   EMPADS

Answer is B. PEMDAS

24. You are helping students list the steps needed to solve the word problem:
   "Mr. Jones is 5 times as old as his son. Two years later he will be 4 times as old as his son. How old is Mr. Jones?"

   One of the students makes the following list:
   1.   Assume Mr. Jones' son is x years old. Express Mr. Jones' age in terms of x.
   2.   Write how old they will be two years later in terms of x.
   3.   Solve the equation for x.
   4.   Multiply the answer by 5 to get Mr. Jones' age.

   What step is missing between steps 2 and 3?
   (Rigorous) (Competency 6)

   A.   Write an equation setting Mr. Jones age equal to 5 times his son's age

   B.   Write an equation setting Mr. Jones age two years later equal to 5 times his son's age two years later

   C.   Write an equation setting Mr. Jones age equal to 4 times his son's age

   D.   Write an equation setting Mr. Jones age two years later equal to 4 times his son's age two years later

Answer: D. Write an equation setting Mr. Jones age two years later equal to 4 times his son's age two years later

25. **The following equation is the best choice for teaching use of the distributive law in solving equations:**
    (Rigorous) (Competency 6)

    A. $3(x + 5) = 4x$

    B. $x(3 + 5) = 4$

    C. $4(x + 2x) = 2$

    D.   None of the above

Answer is A. $3(x + 5) = 4x$
One can apply the distributive law to choice B, but it is simpler to just add 3 and 5 and then multiply by x. One can also apply the distributive law to choice C, but the simpler option is to add x and 2x first and then multiply by 4. To solve choice A, one would have to apply the distributive law $3(x + 5) = 3x + 15$. Hence, A is the best choice.

26. **A student solves the following problem and gets an answer of 45. What is the most likely reason for her mistake?**

    "Sara left for school at quarter to ten and reached there at half past ten. How many hours did it take her to travel to school?"

    (Easy) (Competency 6)

    A.   She does not know what "quarter to" means

    B.   She does not know what "half past" means

    C.   She did not notice that the problem asks for the answer in hours

    D.   She does not know that there are 60 minutes in an hour

Answer: C. She did not notice that the problem asks for the answer in hours

27. **A student does not know how to begin finding the area of the following shape:**

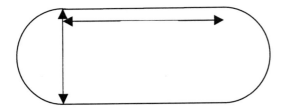

How can a paraprofessional help him to get started?
(Average) (Competency 6)

A.   Ask him to divide the area into a rectangle and two half circles

B.   Tell him to compute $1.5 \times 3 + \pi(0.75)^2$

C.   Ask him whether the shape can be divided into familiar shapes such as rectangles, squares, triangles, and circles

D.   Tell him the formula for the area of a rectangle and the area of a circle

Answer is C. Ask him whether the shape can be divided into familiar shapes such as rectangles, squares, triangles, and circles
The goal of the paraprofessional is to guide the student towards finding his own solution without directly giving too much information.

28. You are helping a group of students identify which of several triangles drawn on a coordinate plane are right triangles. If the coordinates of the vertices are given, the students can identify the right triangles if: *(Rigorous) (Competency 6)*

    A.   They know only the Pythagorean theorem and the distance formula

    B.   They know only the slope formula and the relationship between the slopes of perpendicular lines

    C.   They don't know any of the formulae mentioned in A and B but two legs of the triangle are parallel to the x and y axes.

    D.   All of the above

Answer: D. All of the above
For choice A, they can use the distance formula to find the length of each side of the triangle and then check to see whether they satisfy the Pythagorean theorem. For choice B, they can find the slope of each side of the triangle and check if any two of the sides are perpendicular to each other. For choice C, a triangle with two sides parallel to the x and y axes is necessarily a right triangle.

29. A student is creating a circle graph. Which of these concepts is it absolutely necessary for her to know in order to do the task?

    A.   **Determining the central angle for a sector of the circle**
    B.   **Finding the area of the sector of a circle**
    C.   **Computing percentages**

(Rigorous) (Competency 6)

    A.   A only

    B.   A and B

    C.   A and C

    D.   C only

Answer is A. A only
The area of the sector of the circle is not necessary to draw the circle graph; the central angle is sufficient. Although many circle graphs show percentages, one can create a circle graph without the use of percentages.

30. **A student was asked to find the median of the set of numbers**

"1, 14, 2, 6, 27, 9, 7, 11, 23"

He came up with the answer "27." What was the likely cause of his error?
(Average) (Competency 6)

A.   He did not know what median means and picked a random number

B.   He did not put the numbers in order before identifying the middle number

C.   He picked the largest number

D.   He added up the 3 middle numbers

Answer: B. He did not put the numbers in order before identifying the middle number
Forgetting to put the numbers in order before picking the middle number is a common student error.

Answer Key: Mathematics

1.	B	16.	B
2.	A	17.	D
3.	D	18.	B
4.	C	19.	A
5.	B	20.	D
6.	B	21.	B
7.	C	22.	B
8.	A	23.	B
9.	B	24.	D
10.	D	25.	A
11.	A	26.	C
12.	C	27.	C
13.	D	28.	D
14.	A	29.	A
15.	C	30.	B

Rigor Table: Mathematics

	Easy 20%	Average 40%	Rigorous 40%
Questions	2, 4, 12, 22, 23, 26	1, 3, 6, 9, 11, 15, 16, 17, 19, 21, 27, 30	5, 7, 8, 10, 13, 14, 18, 20, 24, 25, 28, 29

WRITING

Directions: Read the following passage and answer question 1.

Ants have three main parts to their bodies. The first part is the head, which contains the jaw, eyes, and antennae. The second part of an ant's body is the trunk. The trunk has six legs attached to it. The third part of an ant's body is the rear. I was surprised to learn that the rear contains a poison sac. This is one way the ant defends itself.

1. **What type of writing is demonstrated in the passage above?**
   (Rigorous) (Skill 1.7)

   A.   Descriptive

   B.   Narrative

   C.   Expository

   D.   Persuasive

Answer: C. Expository
The passage was written to inform the reader about the parts of an ant's body; therefore, it is expository. Had the author described what they saw when they looked at an ant's body under a microscope, it would be a descriptive passage.

2. **What is the plural of the word _rose_?**
   (Easy) (Skill 1.8)

   A.   Rosis

   B.   Rosses

   C.   Roses

   D.   Rose's

Answer: C. Roses
When making a word that ends in e plural, add an s.

3. **Which word needs to be corrected in the sentence below?**
   (Rigorous) (Skill 1.8)

   The presents on the table is wrapped in beautiful wrapping paper.

   A.   presents

   B.   is

   C.   wrapped

   D.   beautiful

Answer: B. is
Is needs to be replaced with the word *are*. *Is* should be used in the singular form. *Are* is used in the plural form and there is more than one present. Therefore, the sentence should read, "The presents on the table are wrapped in beautiful wrapping paper."

4. **Which sentence is punctuated correctly?**
   (Easy) (Skill 1.8)

   A.   The dog escaped from the house this morning.

   B.   What time will you be home tonight?

   C.   The coffee is very hot!

   D.   I haven't had lunch yet?

Answer: D. I haven't had lunch yet?
A question mark should only be used at the end of a question. Choice D is a statement when it stands alone.

5. **What type of sentence is the sentence below?**
   (Rigorous) (Skill 1.8)

   Jarrett and Austin like to read and write.

   A.   Simple

   B.   Compound

   C.   Complex

   D.   Compound/complex

Answer: A. Simple
The sentence has a compound subject and a compound predicate, but it still consists of one subject and one verb. The conjunction *and* does not join two or more independent clauses so it cannot be a compound sentence.

6. **What must be done to make this sentence correct?**
   (Rigorous) (Skill 1.8)

   Before the children were allowed to go outside.

   A.   Place a comma after before

   B.   Change the word *children* to *child*

   C.   Change the period to a comma and add an independent clause

   D.   Nothing. It is fine the way it is

Answer: C. Change the period to a comma and add an independent clause
This is a dependent clause that needs additional information. Therefore, an independent clause must be added. For example, "Before the children were allowed to go outside, they had to clean their rooms". "They had to clean their rooms" is an independent clause and can stand alone or be proceeded by a dependent clause.

7. **When students just sit down and write about a topic, writing everything that comes to mind, this is called**
   (Average) (Skill 2.6)

   A.   Brainstorming

   B.   Outlining

   C.   Free writing

   D.   Drafting

Answer: C. Free writing
Free writing is a great way to get over writer's block. Students just write about whatever comes to mind for a few minutes. This is a great prewriting strategy.

8. **What is the difference between drafting and revising?**
   (Rigorous) (Skill 2.6)

   A.   Nothing, they are the same thing

   B.   Drafting is the first copy, and revising is the final copy

   C.   Drafting is the first copy and revising corrects spelling errors etc.

   D.   Drafting is the first copy, and revising improves the craft of writing

Answer: D. Drafting is the first copy, and revising improves the craft of writing
Drafting is when students get their ideas down on paper in a semi-coherent piece. Next, students go back and revise their writing to make it better by improving the "craft" of writing.

9. **What is the purpose of editing?**
   (Average) (Skill 2.6)

   A.   To publish a piece of writing for presentation

   B.   To rewrite it in one's neatest handwriting

   C.   To spell check-it in a word processing program

   D.   To check it for spelling, correct punctuation, and grammar

Answer: D. To check it for spelling, correct punctuation, and grammar
Editing is the last step in writing before the piece is ready to be published. This is where the writer checks the spelling, punctuation, and grammar usage.

10. **Students in a classroom are asked to keep a Writer's Notebook that they write in every day. What is the purpose of this notebook?**
    (Rigorous) (Skill 3.6)

    A.   To write down ideas for poems that students might want to write.

    B.   To keep lists of ideas on certain topics that might be developed later.

    C.   To draw quick sketches and then write about them in greater detail.

    D.   All of the above.

Answer: D. All of the above
A Writer's Notebook is a great place to keep prewriting ideas that can later be developed into drafts and perhaps published/finished pieces of writing.

11. Which word best completes the sentence?
   (Easy) (Skill 7.1)

   Maria lost two _____ when she was in kindergarten.

   A.   teeth

   B.   tooth

   C.   tooths

   D.   toothes

Answer: A. teeth
The word *tooth* creates and irregular plural noun. When there is more than one tooth, the correct plural form is *teeth.*

12. Which word will complete the sentence?
   (Average) (Skill 7.2)

   The Johnson's painted _____ house a beautiful shade of yellow.

   A.   they're

   B.   their

   C.   there

   D.   them

Answer: B. their
Their is used to show possession. The house belongs to the Johnsons.

13. **Which word will complete the sentence?**
    (Average) (Skill 7.2)

    We waited _____ long in the movie line.

    A.   too

    B.   to

    C.   two

    D.   tow

Answer: A. too
Too shows extremes or means "also". In this sentence, the wait in the movie line was extremely long.

14. **Jessica asked her brother what time dinner would be ready. He responded by saying, "I could care less". Is Jessica's brother's response correct?**
    (Easy) (Skill 7.2)

    A   Yes

    B.   No

Answer: B. No
Jessica's brother's response is not correct. The correct response is, "I **couldn't** care less".

15. Which word will complete the sentence?
(Rigorous) (Skill 7.3)

That _____ wings are yellow and black.

A.   butterfly's

B.   butterflys'

C.   butterflies

D.   butterflie's

Answer: A. butterfly's
The yellow and black wings belong to one butterfly. Therefore, the correct word is *butterfly's*. Only change "y" to "ie" in the plural.

16. Which sentence is correct?
(Rigorous) (Skill 7.3)

A.   Birds scurrying by to find food in the snow.

B.   Birds scurry by to find food in the snow.

C.   Birds, scurry by to find food in the snow.

D.   Birds scurry by, to find, food in the snow.

Answer: B. Birds scurry by to find food in the snow.
No commas are necessary in these sentences, so choices C and D are incorrectly punctuated. Choice A is a clause and requires more information.

17. **Which punctuation mark is required, if any, in the sentence?**
    (Easy) (Skill 7.3)

    I won't wear plaid stripes, and checks together.

    A.　　!

    B.　　?

    C.　　,

    D.　　None

Answer: C. ,
A comma is necessary between plaid and stripes in order to separate them into two separate ideas. The sentence should read, "I won't wear plaid, stripes, and checks together."

18. **What type of sentence is the sentence below?**
    (Average) (Skill 7.4)

    I was late for the movies but I got popcorn anyway.

    A.　　Simple

    B.　　Compound

    C.　　Complex

    D.　　Compound/Complex

Answer: B. Compound
Two sentences are combined using the conjunction *but.* Therefore, it is a compound sentence.

19. Which sentence is a run-on sentence?
   (Rigorous) (Skill 7.4)

   A.   It was Jill's first day at her new school and she was eager to make friends.

   B.   During lunch Jill sat down at a table Jill ate her sandwich and drank her milk.

   C.   Before long a girl came up and asked Jill if she could sit with her.

   D.   As soon as they began talking Jill knew they would become friends.

Answer: B. During lunch Jill sat down at a table Jill ate her sandwich and drank her milk.
The word Jill is used twice as the subject in this sentence. This sentence can be corrected by inserting a conjunction to join the two independent clauses; *During lunch, Jill sat down at a table and ate her sandwich and drank her milk.* The two dependent clauses can also be separated with a period; *During lunch Jill sat down at a table. She ate her sandwich and drank her milk.*

20. Which change, if any, would make the underlined words correct?
   (Easy) (Skill 7.5)

   I'm sorry that I haven't wrote to you in such a long time.

   A.   haven't written

   B .   haven't writed

   C.   didn't written

   D.   No change necessary

Answer: A. haven't written
The correct past tense form of the verb *to write* that is needed here is *written*.

21. **Which change, if any, would make the underlined word correct?**
(Rigorous) (Skill 7.5)

There are so many characteristics that I like about her, especially the way she cares about the feelings of others and <u>give</u> them her love and devotion.

A.   gave

B.   gives

C.   given

D.   No change necessary

Answer: B. gives
The word has to stay in the same form as the word *care*, which comes before it in the sentence. Gave is past tense, and given could be a past or present participle that must be preceded by the word was or will be.

22. **Which word will make the sentence correct?**
(Easy) (Skill 7.5)

On your way home from work tonight, please stop at the store and pick up some milk, two _____ of bread, and some vegetables for salad.

A.   loafs

B.   loafes

C.   loaves

D.   loavs

Answer: C. loaves
The correct, irregular plural form of the noun *loaf* is *loaves*.

23. **Which sentence is written correctly?**
    (Easy) (Skill 7.5)

    A.   We watched the game, then get tired and gone home.

    B.   We watch the game, then got tired and go home.

    C.   We watched the game, then got tired and went home.

    D.   We watched the game, then get tired and goes home.

Answer: C. We watched the game, then got tired and went home.
The whole sentence is in the past tense. We know this because the main verb *watched* has an -ed at the end. Therefore, the rest of the sentence needs to follow this correctly with all words. The past tense of *to get* is *got*, and the past tense of *to go* is *went*.

24. **Which word will correctly complete the sentence?**
    (Average) (Skill 7.5)

_____ *tails range from breed to breed. Some are very short and curly while others are long and straight.*

    A.   Dogs

    B.   Dogs'

    C.   Dog's

    D.   Doges

Answer: B. Dogs'
The sentence is speaking about many dogs' tails that belong to the dogs. Therefore, the plural form would be *dogs*. Since *dogs* is a possessive noun, the apostrophe comes after the plural *s*.

Directions: Choose the correctly spelled word to complete each sentence for questions 25 to 29.

25. I _____ forget to lock my front door before I leave the house in the morning.
(Average) (Skill 7.6)

   A.   occasionaly

   B.   occasionally

Answer: B. occasionally
The root word is *occasional*. When adding the suffix *–ly*, the *l* becomes doubled.

26. Don't purchase that vehicle unless they offer you a money back _____.
(Average) (Skill 7.6)

   A.   guaruntee

   B.   guarantee

Answer: B. guarantee
Even though the short /u/ sound is heard in the middle of the word, *guarantee* is spelled with an /a/.

27. A prior _____ will cause us to be late to the celebration.
(Average) (Skill 7.6)

   A.   committment

   B.   commitment

Answer: B. commitment
The /m/ is the only doubled letter in the word *commitment*.

28. It is quite an _____ to graduate from high school and continue on to college.
(Average) (Skill 7.6)

   A.   achievement

   B.   acheivement

Answer: A. achievement
The rule *i before e except after c* applies to this word.

29. Due to _____ weather, all after school activities will be cancelled today.
(Average) (Skill 7.6)

   A.   inclement

   B.   inclemet

Answer: A. inclement
The /n/ at the end of the word is often not pronounced and that makes it a difficult word to spell correctly.

30. Before students write a personal narrative, what ideas should be part of their prewriting?
(Rigorous) (Skill 8.1)

   A.   Characters, setting, problem, solution

   B.   The beginning and the ending

   C.   How the piece will be organized. For example, a circle story.

   D.   Sequence of events

Answer: A. Characters, setting, problem, solution
Although all of the choices above will go into planning a personal narrative, students must decide who the characters will be, where the story will take place, what the problem is, and how the problem will be solved. Without these ideas established, it is too likely that the piece will not be focused, and the author will likely get off track in their writing.

31. **If you are helping a student locate information about their state for a research report, what other source can be used besides the Internet?** *(Rigorous) (Skill 8.2)*

    A.   A dictionary

    B.   An atlas

    C.   An almanac

    D.   A thesaurus

Answer: C. An almanac
An almanac is a reference book that gives a lot of information about topics such as a student's state. It may include the state nickname, the state motto and bird, and even some tourist attractions.

32. **When students are writing, which reference book should students use to find synonyms for weak nouns, verbs, and adjectives?** *(Rigorous) (Skill 8.2)*

    A.   A dictionary

    B.   An encyclopedia

    C.   An atlas

    D.   A thesaurus

Answer: D. A thesaurus
A thesaurus is a reference book that students can use to find stronger nouns, verbs, and adjectives that will improve their writing. For example, students can look up the word *nice* and find stronger synonyms that will ultimately improve student writing.

33. **What is another name for a "thesis statement"?**
   (Average) (Skill 8.3)

   A.   A main idea sentence

   B.   An introductory paragraph

   C.   A concluding sentence

   D.   A hook

Answer: A. A main idea sentence
The thesis statement's purpose is to let the reader know what the essay will be about. In other words, it is the main idea of the paper.

34. **How is a five-paragraph essay typically organized?**
   (Average) (Skill 8.3)

   A.   Thesis statement, body, ending thesis

   B.   Introduction, body, conclusion

   C.   Introduction, thesis, conclusion

   D.   Thesis, Introduction, conclusion

Answer: B. Introduction, body, conclusion
Typically, a five-paragraph essay begins with an introductory paragraph that includes the thesis statement, three body paragraphs that begin with a topic sentence, and a concluding paragraph that ties up the essay.

35. **What is the purpose of a topic sentence in the body paragraphs of an essay?**
(Average) (Skill 8.3)

    A.   It states the main idea of the paragraph it begins

    B.   It restates the thesis statement in another way

    C.   It supports an opposing point of view

    D.   It asks a question for the reader to consider

Answer: A. It states the main idea of the paragraph it begins
Each topic sentence of each body paragraph reflects the central idea of the paragraph it introduces. In other words, it states the main idea of the body paragraph it introduces.

36. **What is a good way to edit a paper if it has been handwritten?**
(Rigorous) (Skill 8.4)

    A.   Read the paper backwards

    B.   Have a peer review your paper

    C.   Read the paper aloud

    D.   All of the above

Answer: D. All of the above
By reading the paper backwards, the author is forced to look at every word individually and is more likely to catch spelling errors or incorrect words. Along the same lines, a fresh set of eyes will also catch errors often missed by an author who is too close to the piece. By reading the paper aloud, the author hears where they may have missed inserting the correct punctuation.

37. What are the three reasons that authors write?
(*Average*) (*Skill 8.5*)

    A.   To be graded, to be published, they have to

    B.   To entertain, to inform, to persuade

    C.   To remind, to show, to tell

    D.   To be heard, to be seen, to be noticed

Answer: B. To entertain, to inform, to persuade
Each piece of writing has one of three purposes: to entertain, to inform, or to persuade.

38. How does the audience of the piece effect how it is written?
(*Rigorous*) (*Skill 8.5*)

    A.   The audience of a piece does not effect how a piece is written

    B.   It will determine how long the writing has to be

    C.   The audience will review the writing and give it a grade

    D.   It will determine the language used in the piece

Answer: D. It will determine the language used in the piece
The intended audience of the writing directs if the language used will be formal or informal. If the purpose is to entertain an audience then the language may be somewhat informal. However, if the audience must respond or learn from the writing, it should be written in a more formal manner.

39. **What type of writing has a sequence of events that recounts an event?**
    (Average) (Skill 8.6)

    A.   Persuasive

    B.   Descriptive

    C.   Narrative

    D.   Letter

Answer: C. Narrative
A narrative is story-like, and it recounts or retells events.

40. **If a students wants to write to the principal in an attempt to have the principal change a school rule, which type of writing will the student most likely produce?**
    (Rigorous) (Skill 8.6)

    A.   Narrative

    B.   Descriptive

    C.   Persuasive

    D.   Expository

Answer: C. Persuasive
The student's purpose for writing the letter to the principal is to persuade him/her to take a certain course of action.

Answer Key: Writing

1.	C		21.	B
2.	C		22.	C
3.	B		23.	C
4.	D		24.	B
5.	A		25.	B
6.	C		26.	B
7.	C		27.	B
8.	D		28.	A
9.	D		29.	A
10.	D		30.	A
11.	A		31.	C
12.	B		32.	D
13.	A		33.	A
14.	B		34.	B
15.	A		35.	A
16.	B		36.	D
17.	C		37	B
18.	B		38.	D
19.	B		39.	C
20.	A		40.	C

Rigor Table: Writing

	Easy 20%	Average 40%	Rigorous 40%
Questions	2, 4, 11, 14, 17, 20, 22, 23	7, 9, 12, 13, 18, 24, 25, 26, 27, 28, 29, 33, 34, 35, 37, 39	1, 3, 5, 6, 8, 10, 15, 16, 19, 21, 30, 31, 32, 36, 38, 40

CPSIA information can be obtained at www.ICGtesting.com
Printed in the USA
267330BV00003B/24/P